TALK ABOUT
Drugs

Jacqui Bailey

WAYLAND

First published in 2008 by Wayland

Wayland
338 Euston Road
London NW1 3BH

Wayland Australia
Level 17/207 Kent Street
Sydney, NSW 2000

Editor: Camilla Lloyd
Consultant: Jayne Wright
Designer: Tim Mayer
Picture researcher: Kathy Lockley

Picture acknowledgments: The author and publisher would like to thank
the following for allowing their pictures to be reproduced in this
publication: Cover photograph: Richard Right/Corbis. ACE STOCK
LIMITED/Alamy: 15; Alan Copson City Pictures/Alamy: 26; Andrew
Lichtenstein/Corbis: 24TL; Arthur Turner/Alamy: 20; Bubbles
Photography/Alamy: 45TR; Chapman Wiedelphoto/Photofusion Photo
Library: 40-41; Christ Stewart/ San Francisco Chronicle/Corbis: 24-25;
Corbis: 6B; Creasource/ Corbis: 21; David Hoffman/John Birdsall Social
Issues Photo Library: 33; David Hoffman/Photofusion Photo Library: 16;
David J. Green - Lifestyle/Alamy: 36; David Tothill/Photofusion Photo
Library: 9; Flint/Corbis: 4; Gianni Muratore/Alamy: 6-7T bkg., 14-15B bkg.,
22-23T bkg., 28-29T bkg., 32-33, 38-39T bkg., 44-45B bkg.; Image
100/Corbis: 12; Jack Carey/Alamy: 39T; Janine Wiedel/Photofusion Photo
Library: 27, 29B; Jaubert Bernard/ Alamy:14T; Jennie Woodcock:
Reflections Photolibrary/Corbis: 30; Jeremy Nicholl/Alamy: 38B; John
Birdsall Social Issues Photo Library: 33, 35, 37; John G. Mabanglo/
epa/Corbis: 11; Keith Dannemiller/Corbis: 22TL; Kevin Fleming/Corbis: 5;
Medical-On-Line/Alamy: 34; Paul Doyle/Photofusion Photo Library: 23B;
Rex Features: 13; Richard Wright/Corbis: 43; Somos Images/Corbis: 10;
Steve Klaver/Star Ledger/Corbis: 44T; vario images GmbH & Co.
KG/Alamy: 1, 18-19; Yadid Levy/Alamy: 28TL.

Sources:
BBC: www.bbc.co.uk
Brake: www.brake.org.uk
British Crime Survey on Drug Misuse
Drug Education and Prevention Information Service Review of Drug-
Related Messages Reaching Young People
DrugScope: www.drugscope.org.uk
Home Office Research Study on Drugs and Crime
NHS Information Centre Survey on 'Smoking, drinking and drug use
among young people in England'
UK National Statistics Report on Drug Use, Smoking and Drinking
US National Survey on Drug Use and Health, Department of Health and
Human Services
World Health Organization

British Library Cataloguing in Publication Data:
Bailey, Jacqui
    Talk about drugs
    1. Drug abuse - Juvenile literature
    I. Title II. Drugs
    362.2'9

ISBN: 978 0 7502 4937 9

Printed in China

Wayland is a division of Hachette Children's Books, an
Hachette Livre UK company
www.hachettelivre.co.uk

CONTENTS

Chapter 1

What are drugs?

Did you take a drug today? If you had a headache, your Mum may have given you an aspirin to swallow. Or did you drink a can of cola? If you did either of these things then you were taking drugs.

Harmful or helpful?

A drug is any chemical that affects your body, mind or behaviour. There are thousands of different drugs. Lots of them come from parts of plants. The pain-killing chemical in aspirin, for example, originally came from willow tree bark. However, many more drugs are made in laboratories by chemists.

When people talk about drugs, they usually mean something harmful, dangerous and often illegal (against the law). All drugs can be harmful, and most will kill you if you take them in big enough doses. But many of the same drugs that harm you can also help you — as medicines to treat or prevent illnesses. Whether a drug is harmful or helpful depends on what type of drug it is, how much is taken, how often, and why.

Different drugs

It is not always easy to know if you are taking a drug. The most widely used drug in the world is probably caffeine. Tea, coffee, chocolate, cola and other soft drinks contain caffeine. Caffeine is a stimulant that wakes you up and gives you energy, but if you take too much of it you can end up with a headache, feeling sick, dizzy and unable to sleep.

People drink coffee because the caffeine in it wakes them up. But too much caffeine is bad for your heart and can affect your nerves.

Many drugs come from plants. The tobacco in cigarettes, for example, is farmed in more than 100 countries. The tobacco shown here is being harvested in Tennessee, USA. The United States is one of the biggest tobacco growers in the world.

Millions of people also drink alcohol and smoke cigarettes. In most countries, drugs such as caffeine, alcohol and tobacco are easily available and it is not against the law to take them. However, this doesn't mean that they won't harm you.

Drugs are part of our lives and we all have to find ways of dealing with them. Only you can decide which drugs you will take and which you won't, and to do that you need to find out as much about them as you can.

FACTS

* Coffee is the most popular drink in the world. The USA consumes more coffee than any other country.

* More than half of all the adults in the USA drink about three-and-a-half cups of coffee every day.

* Coffee originally came from North Africa. It first appeared in Europe in the early 1600s.

* Until 2004, caffeine was on the Olympic Committee's list of banned substances.

* A huge dose of caffeine could kill you.

Yesterday and today

Thousands of years ago, people discovered that eating certain plants helped ease their pain or gave them energy. Some even gave them strange dreams! Healers in Ancient Egypt, China, Greece and Rome gave their patients drugs and knew how to turn plants into alcohol.

One of the oldest drugs is opium, which is made from the seeds of a type of poppy. People have used opium for at least 5,000 years. It is a powerful painkiller, but it also affects people's minds, giving them vivid dreams and hallucinations.

In the Middle Ages, people grew herbs for use as medicines and to flavour food. We use many of these herbs in our food and as medicines today.

In the 1800s, cocaine was made into powders, drinks and drops and sold as a miracle cure for all kinds of minor ailments.

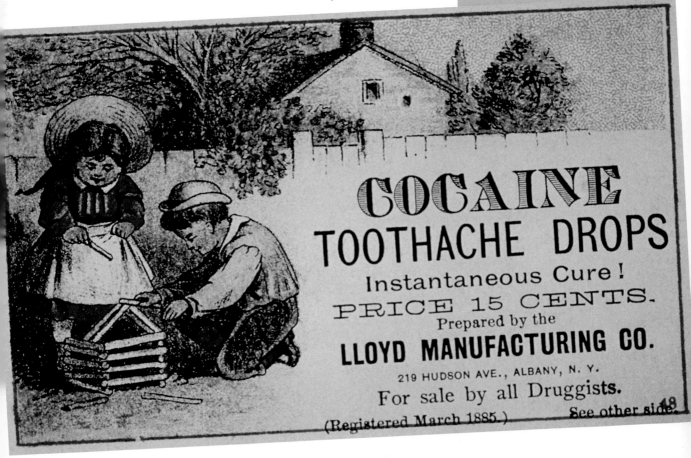

COCAINE TOOTHACHE DROPS

Instantaneous Cure!

PRICE 15 CENTS.

Prepared by the

LLOYD MANUFACTURING CO.

219 HUDSON AVE., ALBANY, N. Y.

For sale by all Druggists.

(Registered March 1885.) See other side.

All over the world

Originally tobacco grew only in America. Tobacco leaves were chewed and smoked by Native Americans, especially in Central and South America. By the 1500s, sailors had brought the habit back to Europe where, at first, it was thought to cure all sorts of illnesses, from toothache to cancer! The fact that tobacco is one of the causes of cancer was only fully realized in the 1950s.

Cocaine is a drug that comes from the leaves of the coca plant, which grows in South America. Chewing the leaves makes people feel strong and energetic and it numbs pain. The Spanish sailors who conquered South America in the 1500s brought the leaves to Europe. It was only at the end of the 1800s that people understood how dangerous the drug was.

In the 1800s, scientists discovered how to separate drugs from the plants that contained them and how to use them to make stronger medicines. The more they learnt about the human body and disease, the more medicines they invented. Most medicines we use today were developed in the past 100 years. Without them, millions would die from infections and diseases. However, the more drugs we have, the more likely it is that some will be used for the wrong reasons.

TALK ABOUT

Imagine what life would be like with no medicines to help us stay healthy.

Think about the millions of people who die each year from using alcohol, tobacco and other drugs.

✳ **Do you think drugs do more harm than good?**

For ideas on how to extend Talk About discussions please see the Notes for Teachers on page 47.

Chapter 2

Why do we take drugs?

People take drugs for all sorts of reasons. They take them because they are ill or in pain or to stop themselves from getting ill. They take them to change themselves in some way – to be slimmer, stronger or more energetic. They take them to relax or to escape from their problems. Or because they think everyone else is taking them and they don't want to be left out.

Take your medicine

There are thousands of different medicines and we use them in all sorts of ways. We take antibiotics to destroy germs that get into our body and infect us. We take painkillers to stop pain, and anaesthetics to prevent us from feeling pain. And we have medicines that treat all kinds of illnesses and diseases, from colds to cancer.

In most countries, many medicines can be bought directly from shops and supermarkets, but for some you need a prescription from a doctor. A prescription is a piece of paper signed by the doctor which lists the name of the medicine, how much of it you need and when you are to take it. You then take the prescription to a chemist or a hospital to get the medicine. Buying or selling prescription drugs without a prescription is against the law.

It happened to me

'I get hay fever and it's always right in the middle of exams. My nose clogs up and my eyes get red and itchy and I just can't think straight. My mum gives me pills for it. They help a bit but it's still pretty bad.'

Josh, 14.

So medicines are safe?

When used properly, medicines help us live longer, pain-free lives. But it's not all good news. Like all drugs, medicines can affect your body in more ways than one. Some of these effects, known as side effects, are uncomfortable or even harmful. Side effects can include headaches, stomach pains, sickness, difficulty breathing and even, sometimes, death.

Our bodies are all different, so different medicines can affect us in different ways. This is why it is never a good idea to take a medicine just to find out what it does. Most can be harmful if they are taken by the wrong person, or if they are mixed with other drugs or taken in large doses. For example, millions of people use paracetamol pills as a painkiller, but taking too many paracetamol at once can damage your liver and may even kill you.

Children all around the world are given vaccination injections to prevent them from catching common illnesses, such as measles and polio.

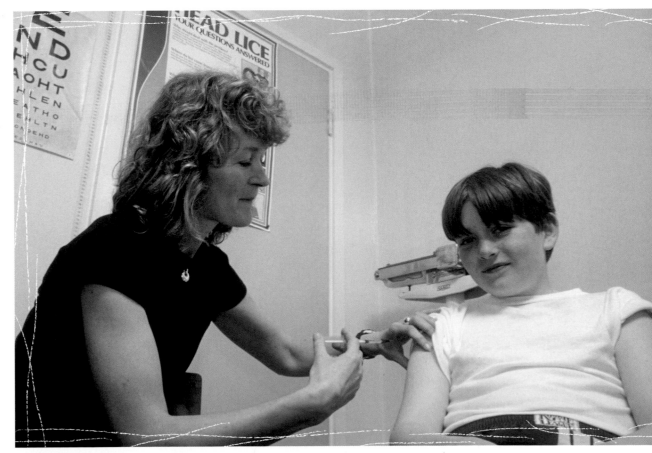

Drugs in sport

Taking drugs has become a big problem in the sports industry. Some athletes take steroid drugs to build stronger muscles. Others take stimulants, such as cocaine or amphetamines to give them more energy. Or they use painkillers or anaesthetics to overcome pain that could slow them down.

Some of these drugs can be bought in shops or with a prescription. Some can only be found illegally. But legal or illegal, they are all prohibited (banned) by the World Anti-Doping Agency. This organization was set up by the International Olympic Committee and other sporting bodies to stamp out the use of drugs in sport. Currently there are about 4,000 drugs banned from use in competitive sport.

Playing fair

Sports organizers believe that taking drugs to improve an athlete's chance of winning is unfair. They regularly test players and competitors to make sure they are not using banned drugs. Anyone who is found using drugs is stopped from taking part in their sport and may have medals, awards or prize money they have won taken from them. Long-term use of sports drugs can also wreck an athlete's health, change their personality and, sometimes, kill them.

Athletes who take drugs say they do it because they are under enormous pressure to win. By winning, athletes can gain a lot of money and fame, but this level of success only lasts for a few years, while they are in top condition.

Steroids build muscle strength, but users can become aggressive and develop severe acne. Men may grow breasts and become sterile, while women's breasts shrink and they grow more facial hair.

Kelli White winning the 200 metres in California in 2003. She later received a two-year ban from the Anti-Doping Agency in the USA.

Looking fit

Some young people see athletes taking drugs and decide to try them too. Some want to find out what the drugs do, or want to make their bodies stronger, or they are encouraged to take them by others. Most do it because they want to be better at sport. Research that was carried out in France among 11 to 15 year-olds showed that almost half of them had tried using drugs at least once to win at sport.

In 2004, 27-year-old world champion runner, Kelli White was banned from running for two years for using steroids and other drugs. She also lost all of the medals and prize money she had won over the previous four years.

Exploring drugs

Do you think that taking drugs sounds cool? Everyone's always talking about them, aren't they? Your parents and teachers say they are dangerous, but lots of celebrities take them and half the people you know say they've drunk alcohol or smoked dope (cannabis), or taken something, and it didn't hurt them. So maybe you should try some, just to see how it feels . . .

People often say they started taking illegal drugs because they wanted to know what it felt like. Or that friends had told them they would 'feel good' or experience a 'buzz'. The problem is that people do not always tell the truth about drugs.

Drugs can give you a 'high' or make you feel sociable but the effects on the body are dangerous. It is a mistake to believe people who say that you need to take drugs to have a good time.

Not what it seems

In spite of what you might think from things you hear or see around you, not everyone tries drugs. Sometimes people say they have tried them when they haven't. And even when people do try drugs, it is not always the great experience they might say it was.

This anti-drug campaign poster shows Leah Betts, who died after taking ecstasy in 1995.

It's true that some drugs can make you feel warm, happy, energetic or confident. But they can just as easily make you feel sick, dizzy, panicky — or worse. Remember, all drugs have a down side. If you are tempted to try an illegal drug, make sure you know what the down side is first.

Solving problems

People may tell themselves that it won't hurt to try drugs 'just once'. Or they are willing to take the risk because they think that drugs will help them cope with their problems.

They may be under pressure at school or at home, or they may not be getting on with their parents, or they may not have much confidence. People also take drugs as a way of escaping violence, abuse, depression or loneliness. For a while, drugs let them pretend that the misery and helplessness they feel is not real. In the end, though, drugs usually cause more problems than they solve.

In the media

Leah Betts was an 18-year-old who died after taking ecstasy (page 33) at her birthday party in 1995. One of the effects of the drug was to make Leah dehydrated. She was so thirsty she drank 7 litres of water in an hour-and-a-half. Drinking so much water so quickly damaged her brain. Leah went into a coma and died three days later.

So what do drugs do?

Drugs change your body, but because our bodies are different, drugs can act on us in different ways. This is especially true if drugs are mixed together or taken with alcohol. If you take too much of a drug – known as an overdose – the effects can be very serious.

Poison

To your body, drugs are poison and need to be cleaned out of your system. If you take the same drug a lot your body gets used to it and becomes faster at getting rid of it. This means that you have to take more of the drug for it to work. This is called having a drug tolerance.

When you stop taking a drug, your body goes through a process known as withdrawal while it gets used to not having the drug.

The side effects of withdrawal from a drug can make you ache all over, feel sick and dizzy, feverish and can give you a blinding headache. They can also make you feel depressed.

Caffeine withdrawal may just give you a headache for a day or two, but withdrawal from other drugs can cause weeks of pain and misery.

Drugs that change your emotions can make you feel calmer, more relaxed, or even intensely happy. This is what people mean when they talk about getting 'high' or getting a 'buzz'. The feeling can be so good that it makes you want to take the drug again, especially if you feel ill or depressed when the first dose wears off. Eventually you might find you cannot do without the drug and have become addicted to it.

Body and mind

Some drugs are more addictive than others. Taking aspirin for a headache won't make you an addict, but you can easily become addicted to taking cocaine. Some drugs are physically addictive, which means your body no longer works normally without them. Others are psychologically addictive, which means that you are emotionally dependent on the drug and cannot enjoy anything without taking it. Often, addicts have both a physical and an emotional need for the drug.

Being an addict means that you have to go on doing the same harmful thing over and over again. Usually addicts need help from trained specialists to break their addiction.

TALK ABOUT

✳ **What reasons might you give for and against taking drugs?**

✳ **If a medicine had serious side effects would you still want to take it?**

✳ **Do you think it is fair on the other sports competitors if some athletes take drugs?**

✳ **Would you believe someone who said it was fun and safe to take drugs?**

Chapter 3

What about drinking and smoking?

You might not realize you have drunk too much until it is too late. Some types of alcohol are stronger than others. And, as everyone's body is different, some people get drunk more quickly than others.

According to the World Health Organization, about two billion people in the world drink alcohol, and one in three people over the age of 15 smokes tobacco. Both drugs are addictive and are a major cause of illness and death.

Why do people drink?

Lots of people drink alcohol socially in pubs or at parties and it is seen as an acceptable thing to do. They feel that alcohol relaxes them, makes them happier or gives them confidence. Some people also drink to escape from their problems, or because they are bored and it's something to do.

In small amounts, alcohol can help keep an adult's heart healthy. But alcohol is addictive and drinking too much of it makes you drunk.

People who are drunk can become aggressive or lose their coordination so that they knock things over and fall about. Their eyesight may become blurred and their speech slurred, and they can find it hard to think clearly. They might be sick and even pass out. People sometimes think that being drunk is funny as it makes people behave stupidly. In fact, being drunk is dangerous and often causes people to harm themselves and others.

Alcopops look and taste like non-alcoholic fizzy drinks, but they have as much alcohol in them as a bottle of beer.

FACTS

* When asked, 21% of 11 to 15-year-olds in the UK said they had drunk alcohol in the previous week.

* Young people aged 14 to 17 who had got drunk said that drinking too much had involved them in accidents, fighting, unsafe sex, taking other drugs and dangerous driving.

* Worldwide, 5% of all the deaths of young people between the ages of 15 and 29 are through alcohol use.

The day after

Being drunk often turns into having a hangover. Hangovers can give you a thumping headache, make you dehydrated, dizzy or sick. You may find it difficult to remember what happened when you were drunk, and you may become depressed.

People who drink a lot can damage their heart, liver and stomach, and can become alcoholics. This means they are physically addicted to alcohol.

In Britain and Australia, it is illegal to buy alcohol or drink it in a club or bar under the age of 18. However, young people can drink alcohol at home below this age. Research in England shows that half of 11 and 12 year-olds who said they had drunk alcohol drank it in their own home or in someone else's.

17

Why smoke?

Cigarettes have been around since the 1700s, but it wasn't until the 1950s that people began to understand how lethal they are. Since then, many governments around the world have been trying to persuade people not to smoke.

Smoking tobacco is not against the law, although in most countries you must be 18 or over to buy it. Tobacco contains around 4,000 different chemicals that affect your body, and the one that is most addictive is nicotine. Smokers say that smoking cigarettes relaxes them and gives them a rush of pleasure, but the only reason they feel pleasure is because nicotine acts on their brain to make them feel that way.

Any pleasure they do get lasts only as long as the cigarette. In return, smokers become short of breath, find it difficult to play sports or be active, damage their skin and teeth, have smelly breath, hair and clothes, damage their heart, risk dying from lung and other cancers, and suffer from a host of other medical problems, from ulcers to loss of eyesight. In fact, according to the World Health Organization, one person dies from tobacco use about every 8 seconds.

One out of two young people in the world who start and then continue to smoke will die of a tobacco-related illness.

TALK ABOUT

Look at these statements about smoking and drinking.
Do you agree or disagree with them?

✳ **People who drink and smoke are seen as 'cool.'**

✳ **Drinking and smoking can relax you and help you have a good time.**

✳ **Smoking is worse than drinking.**

✳ **Smoking and drinking are as bad as each other.**

Why start?

Many people start smoking as teenagers. By the time they are 15, about 20% of young people in England smoke regularly. Many start because they think it will make them look grown up, or they copy those around them, such as their parents or their friends.

Smoking is so addictive that people do not notice that they are gradually smoking more and more. It can then take years of struggle to give up the habit. The good thing about giving up is that as soon as you do, your body starts recovering from some of the damage.

19

Chapter 4

What's the law on drugs?

Because drugs can be so harmful most countries in the world have laws that control the ways in which they are made, sold (or supplied) and used. If you break those laws you have committed a crime and will be punished. How serious the punishment is depends on the type of drug, how much of it there is, whether or not you have been involved with drugs before, whether you are selling drugs and how old you are.

What type?

Although all drugs can do us harm, some are far more likely to damage us than others, either because they are very strong, very addictive or very poisonous — or because they are all of those things! Some drugs are so dangerous that they are not legal in any form. Others might be safe enough if used in small amounts in prescription medicines but lethal in bigger doses, or if mixed with other things.

If you are caught carrying illegal drugs you can be charged with possession, even if the drugs are not yours.

How much?

If you are discovered carrying an illegal drug, you are committing a criminal offence known as possession. If you are carrying a very small amount of the drug and it is your first offence, you might be given a formal warning at a police station. If the drug is one of the more dangerous kinds, or you have been in trouble with drugs before, you could be made to pay a fine, and could be sent to prison.

If you share drugs with your friends, even if you all chipped in the money to buy them, you could be charged with dealing.

If you are carrying enough of the drug for the police to think that you are selling it, or even giving it to someone else, you will be punished much more harshly. Dealers (sellers of illegal drugs) can face long prison sentences, and may spend the rest of their life in prison. In some countries, such as China, Singapore and Thailand, the punishment for drug dealing can even include the death penalty.

FACTS

In the UK, illegal drugs are divided into three groups. Class A drugs are believed to be the most dangerous, so crimes involving these drugs have the toughest punishments.

CLASS A DRUGS

Cocaine and crack

Ecstasy

Heroin

LSD

Magic mushrooms

Methadone

Opium

Any Class B drug that is injected

CLASS B DRUGS

Amphetamines

Barbiturates (sleeping pills)

Codeine (morphine-based painkiller)

CLASS C DRUGS

Cannabis

Mild amphetamines

Some stimulant, anti-depressant and diet medicines

Steroids

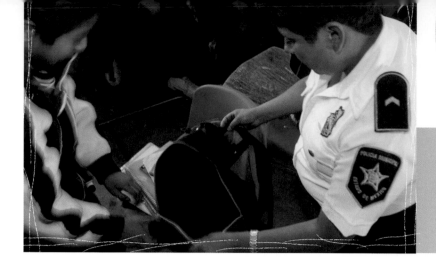

The police can stop and search anyone they think may be carrying an illegal drug. This police officer is searching a teenager's school bag in Mexico.

How old are you?

In the UK, anyone over the age of 10 can be stopped and searched by the police. If you are carrying any illegal drugs, you may be taken to the police station and arrested and charged with possession or dealing. If you are 17 or under, the police must tell your parents or carers what has happened, and must also contact the local youth offending team. This team helps the police and the courts to decide what to do with you.

If you are given a formal warning you might also get a behaviour order (such as an anti-social behaviour order or 'ASBO'). This means you have to agree to obey a particular set of rules for a certain period of time. The rules might include not getting into trouble with the police again or not handling any more drugs. You can be given a behaviour order without being charged.

It happened to me

'I was hanging out with my mates sharing a joint. This cop came round the corner and everyone else legged it, but I wasn't quick enough. I got taken to the police station and locked in a cell. It was horrible and I was really scared. I didn't know what was going to happen and I wanted my mum. Felt like hours, but when she got there she looked really worried and started crying. Made me feel, like, really bad inside.'

Dan, 15.

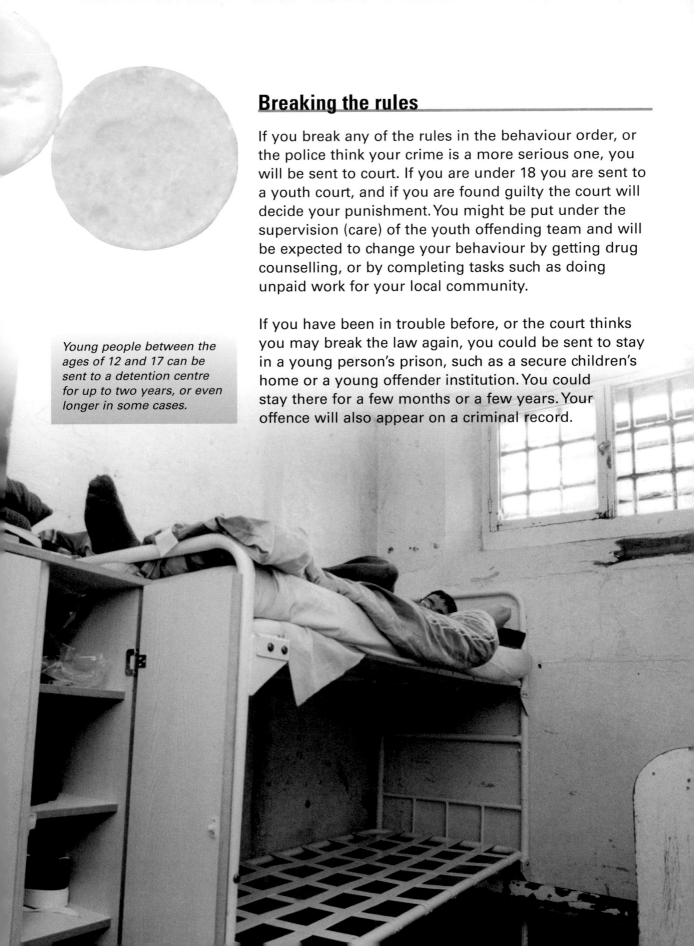

Breaking the rules

If you break any of the rules in the behaviour order, or the police think your crime is a more serious one, you will be sent to court. If you are under 18 you are sent to a youth court, and if you are found guilty the court will decide your punishment. You might be put under the supervision (care) of the youth offending team and will be expected to change your behaviour by getting drug counselling, or by completing tasks such as doing unpaid work for your local community.

If you have been in trouble before, or the court thinks you may break the law again, you could be sent to stay in a young person's prison, such as a secure children's home or a young offender institution. You could stay there for a few months or a few years. Your offence will also appear on a criminal record.

Young people between the ages of 12 and 17 can be sent to a detention centre for up to two years, or even longer in some cases.

Members of the Tactical Narcotics Team in the USA capture a drug dealer. Most police forces have specially trained teams who work on solving drug crimes.

These boys are working in a poppy field in Afghanistan. Opium poppies grow mainly in Thailand, Cambodia, India, Afghanistan and Pakistan. Some opium is grown legally for medicines but most is for the drugs trade.

The drugs trade

Drugs cost money and most people buy them from a dealer. The business of buying and selling illegal drugs is known as the drugs trade. Worldwide, the drugs trade makes around 300 billion US dollars (the equivalent of 146 billion UK pounds) a year.

Most drug users buy their drugs from someone in their local area. Often these dealers use drugs themselves and sell them in order to buy their own.

Dealers get their supplies from wholesalers. Wholesalers are more businesslike about their 'trade' and may or may not take drugs themselves. They deal in large quantities of drugs, and get their supplies from drug traffickers. These are the people who move the drugs from the place where they are grown or made to where they are sold.

Smuggling

Drugs are smuggled into and out of all the countries in the world. For example, cocaine is sent from South America to the USA and Europe. The cannabis sold in the UK comes mostly from the Caribbean, Africa and India. Cannabis sold in the USA, however, is usually grown there.

TALK ABOUT

* **Does anyone benefit from illegal drugs?**
* **Think about the different people involved in the drugs trade. What do you think they might get from it?**
* **Who do you think gets the most from trading in drugs? Who is harmed the most?**

Every time a drug changes hands, its price increases. At one end of the drugs trade are the people growing and making the drugs. These people often work for very low wages because there is no other work they can do. And, because their work is illegal, there is always the chance they could be hurt if they talk about it to an outsider, or if the fields or factories they work in are raided by soldiers or the police.

The owners of the drug farms and factories make their money selling pure forms of the drug to the traffickers. Most traffickers belong to powerful crime gangs, like the Mafia. Traffickers cut the pure drugs down into smaller amounts and mix them with other stuff to make them go further. As the drug is sold on, it is cut and mixed again and again. By the time it reaches the final user it will have increased in cost by ten or even twenty times, and could have been mixed with anything from talcum powder to toilet cleaner.

Chapter 5

What about cannabis?

Cannabis is an illegal drug that comes from the cannabis plant. It is the most widely used of all illegal drugs, particularly by young people. Research carried out among 15-year-old pupils in England shows that, among those who have taken drugs, most have taken cannabis.

Cannabis usually looks like a dried, herby sort of tobacco, or a solid black-ish brown lump known as resin. Both types vary in strength. Resin tends to be stronger than the herb, but there are some very strong types of herbal cannabis, such as skunk and sinsemilla. Cannabis is usually rolled up into a type of cigarette, called a spliff or joint, and smoked. It can also be made into a 'tea' and drunk, or eaten in cakes or other food.

Getting 'stoned'

The kind of experience you get from taking cannabis varies hugely, depending on who you are, the type of cannabis you are using, how you take it, where you take it and who you are with.

Cannabis is made from the leaves, flowers and buds of the cannabis plant.

Cannabis leaves like these can be dried into a tobacco-like herb, or squeezed into solid blocks of resin like the one shown here.

FACTS

Cannabis is also known as:

Hash (hashish)

Ganja

Pot

Reefer

Weed

Spliff

Dope

Bhang

Grass

Skunk

Marijuana

Sinsemilla (sensi)

Wacky baccy

Herb

In general, users say the drug makes them feel relaxed and happy. People who are 'stoned' on cannabis can find things hilariously funny. They might talk a lot, or they might be quiet and withdrawn. Sometimes they think they have found the answer to a huge problem, or have discovered a fantastic idea, but what they say doesn't usually make sense, and later they can't remember what their discovery was. People also get the 'munchies' and might go on an eating binge. Or they may just feel very relaxed and go to sleep.

Cannabis can harm

Cannabis is considered to be a relatively mild drug compared to others. However, that doesn't mean it is harmless. Cannabis can make you feel sick, dizzy and confused. It can affect your judgement and your memory. You might also feel anxious and panicky, or even paranoid (nervous and suspicious of everyone around you). And there is growing evidence that, for some people at least, cannabis can increase the risk of their developing serious mental health problems.

In a few countries, such as the Netherlands, cannabis can be legally used in places like this coffee shop – as long as you are over 18. However, selling or possessing large amounts of the drug is still a crime.

Hooked

Cannabis is not a physically addictive drug, but users can become dependent on it emotionally (psychologically addicted). They find themselves using it more often, spending more money on it and worrying if they run out. Users sometimes can't be bothered to work, feel tired most of the time, don't want to be active or play sport, stop hanging out with friends who don't get stoned, and have rows with their family.

Because cannabis is usually smoked, and often mixed with tobacco, it does as much harm to your body as tobacco. In fact, some scientists say that it does more harm, because cannabis smokers tend to inhale more deeply and for longer. Cannabis users think this will get them more stoned, but all it does is cause even more damage to their lungs.

TALK ABOUT

* **Would making cannabis legal, like alcohol, make it easier to control?**

* **Would making it legal encourage more people to try it and harm more people?**

* **Cannabis is often very strong and can lead to possible mental health problems. Would it be irresponsible to legalize it?**

The big issue

Cannabis is probably the most argued-about drug in the world. In spite of its risks, some people say that it should be legalized in the same way as alcohol and cigarettes. They hope that this will help to keep users, especially young users, from getting involved with more dangerous drugs and the criminals that sell them.

Also, some people with serious illnesses, such as multiple sclerosis, say that cannabis can help to relieve their pain and sickness. Even so, in most countries cannabis is illegal for medicinal use and users risk going to prison. At present, only Canada allows patients to use a medicinal version of the drug.

It's the law

In the UK, in January 2004, cannabis was changed from a Class B drug to a Class C drug (see page 21). This does not mean that it is legal, but that the punishment for possessing or selling it may be less severe than it was. However, people can still be sent to prison for up to 14 years for selling cannabis. Also, while people over 18 might not now automatically be arrested for possessing cannabis, anyone who is under 18 will be taken to a police station and given a formal warning or possibly sent to court (see pages 22–23).

Smoking cannabis carries the same risks and does the same damage to your body as smoking cigarettes.

Chapter 6

What other drugs are there?

Along with cannabis, alcohol and tobacco, the drugs in this chapter are sometimes called 'recreational drugs'. This means that people take them purely to get high with the aim of enjoying themselves. Not all recreational drugs are illegal, but most are.

Sniffing

There are some chemicals that only become 'drugs' when they are used in a certain way. These chemicals are called solvents or 'volatile substances' and they are found in everyday products such as glue, aerosols, lighter fuels, paints, hairsprays and nail polish remover.

Solvents give off fumes which can be breathed in, or 'sniffed'. The fumes give users a 'rush' or 'buzz', making them feel as if they are drunk. Users may hallucinate, become dizzy, sick, confused, sleepy or angry, and they are more likely to take risks.

Solvents can be very dangerous. There is no way of knowing how your body will react to a solvent, whether it's the first or the fifteenth time you've used it.

Danger zone

Sniffing solvents is incredibly dangerous. You can pass out and then be so sick that you choke on your own vomit. Solvents can make your heart race so strongly that it can't cope and just stops, killing you instantly.

Sniffing solvents with your head inside a plastic bag, or squirting them directly into your throat can suffocate you. And, because solvents catch fire very easily, you may accidentally burn yourself or set yourself on fire. Between 70 to 100 people in the UK die from solvents every year — that's more than one person a week. In the USA, experts estimate that several hundred people die from solvent abuse every year.

It is not illegal to buy or own products that contain solvents, and such things are found in most homes. This makes their use as a drug difficult to control. But it is because they are so easy to get hold of that solvents are mostly used by young people, especially 11 to 15 year-olds. In the UK, research shows that 11 and 12 year-olds are more likely to try solvents than cannabis.

FACTS

* **One third of young people killed by solvents are first-time users.**
* **Over half the deaths from solvent sniffing are caused by the poisons in the chemicals themselves.**
* **Other deaths are caused by choking, suffocation or accidents that occur while the drug is being used.**
* **Long-term solvent abuse can cause depression and damage your brain, liver, kidneys and nervous system.**

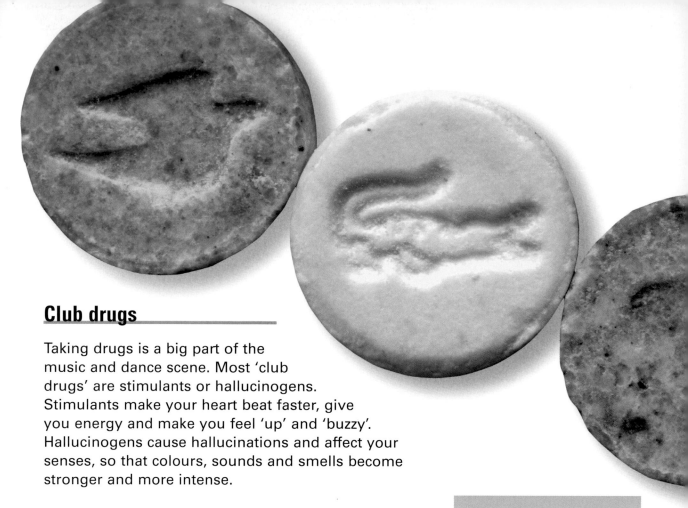

Club drugs

Taking drugs is a big part of the
music and dance scene. Most 'club
drugs' are stimulants or hallucinogens.
Stimulants make your heart beat faster, give
you energy and make you feel 'up' and 'buzzy'.
Hallucinogens cause hallucinations and affect your
senses, so that colours, sounds and smells become
stronger and more intense.

Ups and downs

Poppers, amphetamines and methamphetamine are
stimulants. Poppers are liquids with strong fumes that
are breathed in to give an instant rush. Inhaling
poppers can make you feel sick, dizzy, or pass out.
Sniffing poppers can be fatal for anyone with heart or
breathing problems. They can cause rashes around the
mouth and nose, and the liquid burns if it gets on your
skin and will kill you if swallowed.

Amphetamines (such as speed and uppers), and the
more powerful methamphetamine (crystal meth), are
stronger than poppers. They are sold as powders, pills,
or a soft putty, and are usually sniffed or swallowed.
The effects can last for up to eight hours, leaving users
exhausted and depressed when they wear off. They are
addictive and, if taken often or in large doses, can make
people anxious, irritable or paranoid, and sometimes,
aggressive. They can give you brain damage, harm
your heart and can kill you if mixed with other drugs.

*Ecstasy pills may look
pretty, but they are often
heavily cut with anything
from laxatives to cleaning
powder, or mixed with
cheaper drugs, such
as ketamin (an anaesthetic).
The danger is that you
never know what you
are swallowing.*

Poppers are little bottles or tubes of clear or yellow liquid, with names such as Liquid Gold, TNT or Rave. They are often sold as 'video-head cleaners' or 'room deodorizers'.

Ecstasy

Ecstasy (MDMA) is the most famous club drug. It works like an amphetamine but is also mildly hallucinogenic. Users say it makes them feel warm and happy, but some people have a bad reaction to it and get nervous, confused or panicky. Ecstasy makes your body heat up and your heart race. Ecstasy users can dance for hours, but then they get even hotter and dehydrate (lose a lot of body water). Overheating and dehydration can lead to brain or heart damage and death. Long-term use of ecstasy can cause permanent brain damage.

DOs & DON'Ts

If one of your friends has taken ecstasy:

✳ **Get them to drink lots of water, but make sure they drink it slowly, about 500ml (1 pint) every hour. Drinking too much too quickly can be just as dangerous as not drinking enough.**

✳ **If your friend starts to look ill or passes out, stay with them but get help and call an ambulance.**

✳ **Never drink alcohol while taking drugs.**

✳ **Don't let anyone who has taken ecstasy dance non-stop. Make sure they take regular breaks from dancing so their body has a chance to cool down.**

Seeing things

Getting high on stronger hallucinogenic drugs, such as LSD (acid) and 'magic mushrooms' is known as 'tripping'. A trip can last for 12 hours or more. It is impossible to control the effects and every trip is different. A trip may be amazing or truly terrifying.

The hard stuff

The most highly addictive drugs get users hooked and steal their lives. The worst of these are cocaine, crack and heroine.

Cocaine (also called C, coke, charlie, snow, blow) is a white powder made from the coca leaf. It is sniffed through a rolled-up paper or a straw, or rubbed inside the mouth, or mixed with a liquid and injected.

A tiny drop of LSD on a small square of blotting paper, known a 'tab', is enough for one trip. A bad trip can cause mental damage and users may get flashbacks for days afterwards.

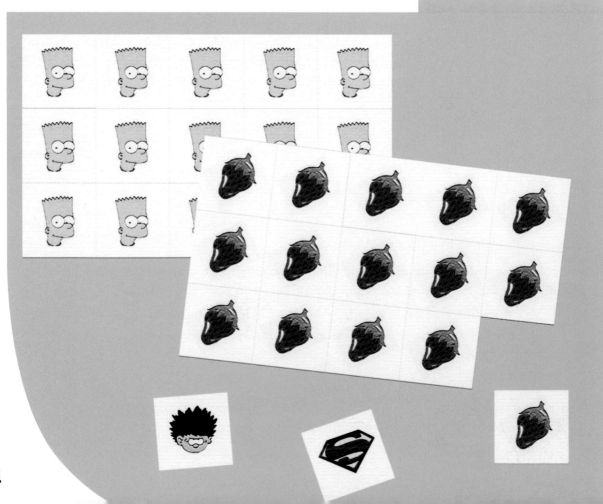

Cocaine and crack are expensive and taking them has become 'fashionable' among some celebrities and the super-rich. Taking too much can cause fits, heart failure and death.
These drugs are even more dangerous if used with alcohol.

Crack is cocaine that has been turned into small lumps or 'rocks'. It is usually heated so the fumes can be breathed in. It gives users a huge 'rush' of energy and confidence. The rush never lasts long, so people take it again and again. Regular use can cause depression, anxiety and panic attacks.

Heroin (H, horse, brown, smack) is a drug made from opium. It is normally an off-white or brown powder that is smoked, injected or sometimes sniffed. Heroin users quickly build up a tolerance to the drug and have to take more and more just to feel 'normal' and avoid the agony of withdrawal. Heroin blocks out pain and sadness and makes people feel warm and relaxed. But when it wears off users feel worse than they did before.

People die from overdosing on heroin and cocaine, and from mixing them with alcohol or other drugs.

In the blood

Users often inject these drugs and tend to share the needles and syringes. Blood from one person's body can get onto the needle and deadly diseases such as HIV/AIDS and hepatitis can be passed on to the next user.

TALK ABOUT

✳ **Do you think people who take drugs really enjoy themselves more than those who don't? Or do you think this is just an effect of the drugs they have taken?**

✳ **Are the health effects and the feelings the next day worth the temporary 'high'?**

Chapter 7

Paying the price

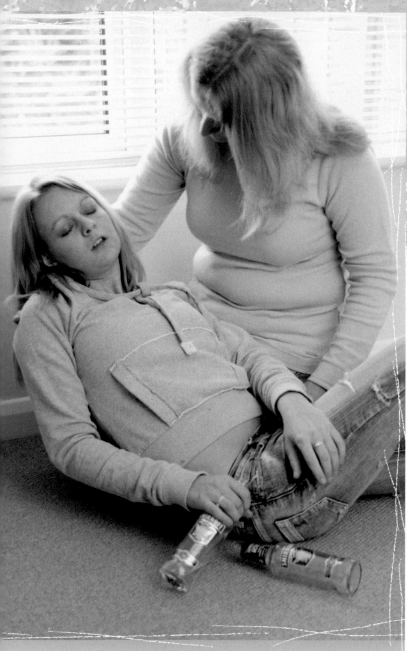

More and more young people are suffering from liver damage and other long-term health problems because of drinking too much alcohol.

Drugs can cost users a lot more than just money. Becoming addicted to drugs such as alcohol, tobacco, cocaine or heroin, for example, physically changes you so that your body wants endless supplies of the drug. It's like always feeling hungry, no matter how much you eat!

Even when drugs are not physically addictive they can be psychologically addictive. At first they can seem to make people's lives easier or better, so it is hard to stop taking them and the drug-taking becomes a habit. Then it becomes something the user needs just to help them get through the day. At this point, they have become addicted to it.

Out of control

Addicts no longer control their own lives, instead they are controlled by their drug. Smokers find it difficult to concentrate without having a cigarette, and may get bad tempered if they can't smoke. But they are usually able to get on with their lives more or less normally.

Drugs such as alcohol, cocaine or heroin can change someone's personality completely, making him or her moody, aggressive, unreliable, uninterested in anything else and hard to talk to. People addicted to these drugs may feel ashamed or guilty, so they hide their habit from their family or friends and often tell lies about what they do and where they go.

Trapped

If addicts run out of money for drugs, they might even start stealing from their family or friends. They stop caring about their studies or their job, and can even stop caring about the people they love. Eventually, long-term addicts can push everyone so far away from themselves that they find they are left with nothing but the drug.

Usually addicts are very unhappy and hate what they are doing, but they are trapped by their need for the drug and cannot stop themselves taking it.

It happened to me

'My best friend's an addict. Well, she's not really my best friend now because we don't see each other any more. She changed. She used to be really good fun and we had all sorts of plans for things we were going to do. Then she stopped wanting to do anything except go off with her druggy mates. She didn't care about me at all. I still miss her though.'

Alice, 16.

Affecting others

Addicts don't only hurt themselves; they often damage the lives of everyone around them. Parents can become ill with anxiety over what is happening to their child. Other children in the family can be left feeling worried, depressed, and angry towards their whole family.

If the parents are addicts, their children may end up having to care for their parents as well as themselves. Or they may be neglected or abused by their parents, and may end up in a care home or foster home. Even worse, the children might start taking drugs too, because seeing their parents do it makes them think it is a normal thing to do.

The driver of this car in Moscow was drunk when it went off the road. People who drive while they are drunk or high on drugs do not only risk killing or damaging themselves, but others as well.

The victims of crimes such as mugging may be physically hurt and are often left feeling helpless, angry and frightened.

In the neighbourhood

Drugs can make people behave in violent and risky ways. Research in the USA has shown that people who take drugs are more likely to commit crimes than those who don't, and that many criminals are found to be high on drugs when they carry out crimes. Sometimes crimes such as mugging, theft or burglary are committed to get the money to pay for drugs.

The drugs trade is mostly run by tough and violent criminal gangs, who fight with each other as well as the police. People, including innocent bystanders, can be injured or killed in drug wars.

But it would be wrong to think that all criminals are drug takers, or that all drug takers commit crimes. Even when addicts do commit crimes they are not necessarily bad people. Most have become addicts because they are trying to escape from some other problem in their lives. Once they are hooked, the drug itself is often a far greater problem than any they had before.

In the media

According to a press release from Brake, a road safety charity in the UK, as many as one in five 17 to 18-year-old drivers in the UK admits to driving after drinking or taking drugs. And one in three of those questioned said they had been in a car driven by a drunk or drugged driver. Government figures show that as many as four 17 to 18-year-olds are killed or injured in car crashes in the UK every day.

What happens to drug addicts?

At some point, every addict has to face up to their drug problem and try to break free of it, because sooner or later their addiction will probably kill them. Curing an addiction can take a huge amount of effort and needs lots of help and support from other people.

Step by step

The first step is often the hardest, because the user has to admit to themselves and to other people that they have a drug problem and that they seriously want to do something about it. Without this, nothing else will work. You cannot force another person to give up drugs but you can help them to do it.

The next step is to talk to someone they trust, like a friend or a parent, who will help them find the professional advice they need. A local doctor or hospital is a good place to start, or there are agencies and organizations that can give advice over the phone, by e-mail, or in person (see page 47.)

Drug treatment

The sort of treatment needed depends on the person, the drug and the reason for their addiction. It might include advice and support on drug use and how to gradually stop using the drug.

Or an addict may be given help to stop taking the drug altogether and go through withdrawal while their body cleans it out of their system. This is known as detoxification ('detox'), and might mean living in a special hospital unit, or a rehabilitation ('rehab') clinic for a while. Sometimes people stay in rehab clinics for weeks or even months.

An addict may be given counselling or some other kind of therapy to help them work out the reasons why they became an addict in the first place, and to give them the emotional strength to stay off the drug.

The aim of drug treatment is not only to help people give up drugs, but also to help them take back control of their own lives. Addicts may need help finding a home, or getting job training or an education.

TALK ABOUT

* Who do you think suffers most from drug addiction?

* How would you feel if a member of your family was an addict?

* What about the rest of us? Caring for addicts in hospitals and treatment centres costs the country a lot of money. And what about the victims of drug-related crimes?

Chapter 8

It's your choice

Most people live their lives without feeling that they need to use drugs — at least, not illegal ones. And although some young people drink alcohol, smoke or try cannabis, very few try Class A drugs.

However you feel about illegal drugs, at some point or other you are going to come into contact with them. You might be offered some by a friend, or you might think about buying some just to find out what the fuss is all about. You might even have tried some already. It's your choice. Whether you do or don't do drugs, the best and safest way to treat them is to make sure you get as much accurate information about them as you can — and not just from your friends.

Check it out

Reading this book is a good start, but there are lots of other books with different information in them. Have a look in your school or public library. Talk to your parents and teachers. Ask them if you can go online to some of the websites that give you straightforward facts and advice about drugs, alcohol and smoking (see page 47). Then you can make up your own mind.

FACTS

* **About one in three people aged between 16 and 59 in England and Wales has used one or more illegal drugs at some time.**

* **More people use cannabis than any other illegal drug.**

* **People are most likely to take illegal drugs between the ages of 16 and 24.**

* **By the time they reach their mid to late 20s, most people have stopped or cut back on using illegal drugs, and most drink less alcohol.**

You can say **no** to drugs. This does not mean you can't hang out with your friends.

What the papers say

Some stories in newspapers and magazines are about celebrities who are taking drugs. The stories are often written as if the information they give is shocking, yet at the same time they make it seem as if drug-taking is a glamorous thing. If the story is not about a celebrity, then it is likely to be about drug crime. These sorts of stories can make it seem as if all users who aren't celebrities are drug-crazed criminals. The stories are dramatic and exciting, but they only show one point of view. The papers rarely feature stories about ordinary people and their problems with drugs.

Getting the message

Governments give people information about the risks of drug-taking. They run advertising campaigns, produce books and leaflets and try to make sure that drug information is taught in schools. By doing this they are hoping to stop people from using drugs or persuade them to cut back on their drug-taking.

These young people are learning about drugs from the National Guard Counter-Task Force in Vernon, USA.

Drugs in schools

In the past, most of the information given to young people in school tended to focus on the fact that all drugs are dangerous. The message was simple: 'Just Say No!'

However, not all drugs have the same level of danger, and young people need to be given as much information as possible about each type of drug and its effects.

Many schools are finding that pupils welcome the chance to have open discussions about drugs, where they can learn to form their own opinions by listening to others. Some schools invite people with first-hand experience of drugs to talk to their students.

Sometimes, these people are ex-addicts or the parents of drug-users, or those who work with addicts. If your school doesn't do this, perhaps you and your friends could try suggesting it to your teachers.

Face up to it

The most important thing of all is for young people to be willing to listen and think about the information they are given. We all need to face up to the fact that drugs are not a quick answer to our problems or an easy way to have a laugh. We need to recognize that there are real reasons for staying away from them. They can and do wreck people's health and lives.

People who take drugs often say that they began taking them when they were in school or college. So the more information you have about them now, the better equipped you will be to make the right choices. You will also be less likely to let other people persuade you to try them. Remember, it really is your life, so think for yourself first and don't be just another drugs victim.

There are so many great things to do with your life, don't waste it on drugs.

TALK ABOUT

* Do you think drugs education makes a difference to whether or not people take drugs? Even if it doesn't stop people from trying drugs, might it help them to use drugs more safely?

* What sort of drugs education would you like to have?

Glossary

alcohol A colourless liquid that makes people drunk, also known as ethanol. It is found in drinks such as beer, cider, wine and spirits such as whisky, gin and vodka.

anaesthetics A group of drugs that make the taker unable to feel pain. An anaesthetic may be inhaled as a gas or injected as a liquid. It can be used to make a part of the body feel completely numb, or to put someone to sleep before an operation.

arrest To take someone to a police station and keep them there until they have been charged with a crime.

aspirin A pill or powder usually used to treat mild pain and fever.

charge To be formally accused of a crime.

dependent To be physically or emotionally unable to do without a particular thing or person.

dose A particular amount of a drug taken in one go.

fine An amount of money that someone is ordered to pay to a court as a punishment for breaking the law. You can be sent to prison for failing to pay a fine.

germs Tiny life forms that cannot be seen without a microscope. Germs can make us ill if they get inside our body.

hallucinations Seeing or hearing things that appear to be real but are not.

injection Putting a drug into someone's body by using a syringe fixed to a hollow needle. The needle is pushed into a muscle or a vein and the plunger at the other end of the syringe is pushed down to force the drug out of the syringe and into the body.

law The set of rules that each country has that limits the ways in which its people can behave. People may be punished for breaking a law.

offence Breaking a law.

solvent Any liquid that is used to dissolve something else to form a liquid mixture. Most solvents are used to make cleaners, paint thinners, glues and perfumes.

sterile Not able to produce children.

syringe A small plastic tube with a plunger at one end. The other end is usually fixed to a hollow needle so that liquid in the syringe can be pushed from the tube through the needle.

tobacco A plant with leaves that are dried and smoked or chewed. Tobacco contains a poisonous chemical called nicotine. Nicotine is as addictive as heroin and cocaine.

World Health Organization The part of the United Nations that checks on the levels of health and welfare in all countries of the world and works to improve them.

Further information

Notes for Teachers:

The Talk About panels are to be used to encourage debate and avoid the polarization of views. One way of doing this is to use 'continuum lines'. Think of a range of statements or opinions about the topics that can then be considered by the pupils. An imaginary line is constructed that pupils can stand along to show what they feel in response to each statement (please see above). If they strongly agree or disagree with the viewpoint they can stand by the signs, if the response is somewhere in between they stand along the line in the relevant place. If the response is 'neither agree, nor disagree' or they 'don't know' then they stand at an equal distance from each sign, in the middle. Alternatively, continuum lines can be drawn out on paper and pupils can mark a cross on the line to reflect their views.

Books to read

Emotional Health Issues: Alcohol and Drug Abuse by Paul Mason (Wayland, 2008)

Know the Facts: Drinking and Smoking by Sarah Medina (Wayland, 2008)

Know the Facts: Drugs by Jillian Powell (Wayland, 2008)

Websites and helplines

ASH (Action on Smoking and Health)

A public health charity that campaigns to reduce the harm caused by smoking. Gives lots of information and statistics about tobacco and smoking, and advice on how to give up.
Website: www.newash.org.uk

ChildLine

A free advice and information helpline for any child or young person who needs someone to talk to.
Website: www.childline.org.uk
Phone: 00 44 (0)800 1111
(Free 24-hour helpline)

Children's Legal Centre

A charity providing free legal advice and information about the laws that affect children and young people.
Website: www.childrenslegalcentre.com

Connexions Direct

Gives information and advice to teenagers on everything to do with health, money, housing or school problems, finding work, relationships and lots more. Their advisers can be contacted by phone (free from landlines or will call you back on your mobile), text, e-mail via website, or online.
Website: www.connexions-direct.com
Phone: 00 44 (0)80 800 13219
Text: 00 44 (0)77 664 13219

Drugsline

An independent helpline offering advice and counselling to anyone with a drug or alcohol problem and their families. They also give talks to schools and parents.
Website: www.drugsline.org
Phone: 00 44 (0)808 1 606 606
(Free 24-hour helpline)

DrugScope

An independent charity giving a vast amount of information on everything to do with drugs, including drugs education, treatment, government policy and the law. The site also contains DrugSearch, an online encyclopedia of drugs, their history and their effects.
Website: www.drugscope.org.uk

D-World

Is DrugScope's website for 11 to 14-year-olds. It contains video stories, fact files for all the main drugs, a photo gallery, games and ideas for projects. It also includes information for parents and teachers.
Website: www.drugscope-dworld.org.uk

FRANK

A government supported website designed to give information and advice on drugs to young people. As well as detailed information on specific drugs, FRANK has news articles, true-life stories, a chat forum where you can share your ideas, and offers confidential help and advice by phone, e-mail (via the website) or online.
Website: www.talktofrank.com
Phone: 00 44 (0)800 77 66 00
(Free 24-hour helpline)

Index

TALK ABOUT

Contents of titles in the series:

Bullying

978 0 7502 4617 0
1. Let's talk about bullying
2. What is bullying?
3. How does it feel to be bullied?
4. Who gets bullied?
5. Why do people bully?
6. Beating bullying
7. Bullying in society

Eating Disorders and Body Image

978 0 7502 4936 2
1. What are eating disorders?
2. Food and the body
3. What does it mean to have an eating disorder?
4. Who gets eating disorders?
5. What causes eating disorders?
6. Preventing problems
7. The treatment of eating disorders

Racism

978 0 7502 4935 5
1. What is racism?
2. Why are people racist?
3. What do racists do?
4. Hidden racism
5. What is religious prejudice?
6. Racism against migrants
7. Nazi racial policies
8. What can we do about racism?

Drugs

978 0 7502 4937 9
1. What are drugs?
2. Why do we take drugs?
3. What about drinking and smoking?
4. What's the law on drugs?
5. What about cannabis?
6. What other drugs are there?
7. Paying the price
8. It's your choice

Homelessness

978 0 7502 4934 8
1. What is homelessness?
2. Why do people become homeless?
3. Homelessness and children
4. Addiction and homelessness
5. Staying clean and healthy
6. Mental health
7. Working and earning
8. Helping the homeless

Youth Crime

978 0 7502 4938 6
1. What is crime?
2. Crime past and present
3. Why does youth crime happen?
4. Behaving badly
5. Crimes of theft
6. Crimes of violence
7. What happens if you commit a crime?
8. What can you do about crime?

WAYLAND